The Fabian Society

The Fabian Society is Britain's leading left of centre political society, committed to creating the political ideas and debates which can shape the future of progressive politics.

With over 300 Fabian MPs, MEPs, Peers, MSPs and AMs, the Society plays an unparalleled role in linking the ability to influence policy debates at the highest level with vigorous grassroots debate among our growing membership of over 7000 people, 70 local branches meeting regularly throughout Britain and a vibrant Young Fabian section organising its own activities. Fabian publications, events and ideas therefore reach and influence a wider audience than those of any comparable think tank. The Society is unique among think tanks in being a thriving, democratically-constituted membership organisation, affiliated to the Labour Party but organisationally and editorially independent.

For over 120 years Fabians have been central to every important renewal and revision of left of centre thinking. The Fabian commitment to open and participatory debate is as important today as ever before as we explore the ideas, politics and policies which will define the next generation of progressive politics in Britain, Europe and around the world. Find out more at **www.fabian-society.org.uk**

Fabian Society
11 Dartmouth Street
London SW1H 9BN
www.fabian-society.org.uk

" Fabian ideas
Series editor: Ellie Levenson

First published March 2004

ISBN 0 7163 0610 7
ISSN 1469 0136

This book, like all publications of the Fabian Society, represents not the collective views of the Society but only the views of the author. This publication may not be reproduced without express permission of the Fabian Society.

British Library Cataloguing in Publication data.
A catalogue record for this book is available from the British Library.

Printed by Bell & Bain, Glasgow

Contents

Introduction	1
1 | The accountability jungle	4
2 | Voice and choice	15
3 | Public Service Guarantees	25
4 | Conclusion	35

About the authors

Tony Wright is Labour MP for Cannock Chase and chair of the Public Administration Select Committee. He is also chair of the Centre for Public Scrutiny. His latest book is *British Politics: A Very Short Introduction* (Oxford University Press, 2003).

Pauline Ngan was formerly researcher to Tony Wright and research officer at Democratic Audit, University of Essex. She is co-author (with David Beetham, Iain Byrne and Stuart Weir) of *Democracy under Blair*, (Politico's, 2002).

Acknowledgements

We would like to thank Kate Lloyd for providing research assistance that greatly benefited the development of this pamphlet. We are also grateful to the anonymous readers of our draft, whose valuable comments we have reflected on if not always acted on.

Introduction

Let us start this discussion of public service reform with three paradoxes, if only to get the intellectual juices going.

Paradox One: In early Fabian propaganda, at the end of the nineteenth century, there was a favourite argument designed to show the inefficiency of choice and competition in the provision of basic services. This involved pointing to the succession of milk, coal and bread carts which delivered their wares in a particular street, each stopping at different houses. There could be no more vivid illustration in Fabian eyes of the wasteful inefficiency of the market model and of the need to replace such chaos with the organisational logic of collectivism. Yet now, a century or so on, the progressive public service agenda is busily exploring how the alleged virtues of choice and competition can be inserted into the provision of collectivised public services.

Paradox Two: There is one public service in which Britain is universally acknowledged to be a world leader. It is regularly called upon to display its professionalism and efficiency, especially at moments of crisis and emergency. It has sharp lines of accountability, a clear mission, wide public respect and is untainted by the charge of producer interest. The service in question is, of course, the armed forces. The idea of Britain having a public service that is best in class internationally sits at odds with the country's reputation as Europe's public service basket case. It also provides a standing refutation of those who argue, ideologically, that the state is incapable of providing public services that work.

A New Social Contract

Paradox Three: It used to be common for those employed by the state to describe themselves as 'public servants'. Indeed, there was a time when railway workers would refer to themselves as 'railway servants'. There could scarcely be a better example than this of the power of a public service ethos, the pride in working for the state in the service of citizens and the sense of duty that this carried with it. Except for the fact that the heyday of the railway 'servant' was the pre-nationalisation era of the old GWR and its sister companies, although it was certainly carried over into the nationalised railway (but may not have survived privatisation). This suggests that it is unwise simply to conflate a public service ethos with a public sector ethos.

But enough of preliminary paradoxes. Our aim here is to carry the argument about public service reform forward. It seems to have become rather stuck, with a number of different (and sometimes competing) approaches in evidence. We briefly discuss some of these, but our main purpose is to suggest a new direction of travel. This builds on some current initiatives, as well as on the experience of the 'Citizen's Charter' from an earlier period, and involves coming at public service reform from a distinctive angle. The Government's approach has hitherto been characterised by central target-setting, sometimes as a kind of shock therapy for service providers. There is now evidence of a reaction against this, and a developing understanding that durable reform will require other approaches.[1]

In a nutshell, the approach we offer turns public service reform on its head. We want to put public service users in the driving seat. This involves a radical break from the top-down managerialism of targetry (although target-setting by organisations is a feature of good management everywhere). We think people are entitled to know what they can expect for the money they pay for their public services, in as precise a way as possible, and to know what happens if such expectations are not fulfilled. Public services represent a contract between the state and its citizens, and the terms of that contract need to be specified more explicitly. We introduce the idea of Public Service Guarantees to describe

Introduction

what we have in mind. This involves a shift from deliverer to user, and from targets to entitlements.

1 | The accountability jungle

Changing public services

There will be immediate objections to this approach, and not just from the familiar nay-sayers who manage to combine a general endorsement of the need for public service reform with instinctive opposition to any specific proposal that disturbs established interests. Some will see the emphasis on users as an embrace of consumerism that dissolves the notion of citizenship. Much nonsense is talked (and written) on this subject. Sometimes it seems to be suggested that, as public services are embodiments of a common citizenship, it is either irrelevant or damaging to suggest that they should attend to consumer considerations. It is doubtful if actual citizens are attracted to this view. There is nothing in the idea of citizenship that prevents public services applying good consumer principles in the way they operate, or giving more power to users. It is far more likely that state services will nourish the bonds of citizenship if they display these attributes.

Of course consumerism (or user-ism) is not enough. If it was then we would let the criminals run the prisons. A public interest may have to be asserted over private interests, needs as well as wants taken into account, and the position of future users as well as current ones considered. This is why we have public services, and why we run them by mechanisms of collective democratic choice. However, none of this prevents us exploring ways in which public service users can have more

The accountability jungle

say, or more rights. To suggest that it does is simply an intellectual and political cop-out. If it is coupled with a defensive protectiveness about the existing mechanisms of collective democratic choice, it becomes a double cop-out.

There is also a fear that going too far down the user road will end in the break-up of public services, or at least to the erosion of key public service principles such as equity and access. This is the legitimate charge against Conservative proposals to fund exit routes from public provision in health and education, not only involving a huge deadweight cost as public subsidy goes to those who do not need it but also reflecting an ideological animus against public provision itself. The *Financial Times* offered this analysis: 'Patients spend about £3 billion a year in private hospitals. Allowing them to take 60 per cent of the cost of NHS treatment would be likely to result in a deadweight cost of more than £1 billion. And in practice the subsidy would not cover 60 per cent of the cost of private treatment, not least because the Conservative proposal would inflate the price of private care.'[2] However, those who properly point this out are not thereby relieved of the obligation to come up with their own proposals to overcome the disabilities of monopoly providers from the perspective of users.

There is a fundamental issue, which we are not able to explore at length, about the drivers of change in public services. If a private company fails to satisfy its customers, it will eventually lose those customers and go out of business. If a state organisation fails to satisfy its users, it will continue to operate for as long as the public money keeps flowing. The electorate may get restless, pushing public services to the top of the national political agenda and punishing those who fail to deliver improvements (which is not the same, by the way, as rewarding those who do, as expectations also change). Yet this is a blunt instrument. It has also been generally ineffective at a local level, where the infirmities of local democracy have routinely enabled poor providers to escape electoral retribution (although there are preliminary indications from local elections that the Comprehensive Performance

Assessment process may be beginning to have some impact on electoral outcomes, which would be a very significant development).

Then there are the internal drivers of change and improvement, including an ethos of public service and professionalism. These are crucial, and should not be underestimated; but the other face of professionalism is a defence of vested interests. State organisations, and those who work in them, can become interests in their own right, to be expanded, defended and protected even at the expense of those for whom state services are provided and who would benefit from changes in the way they operate. This is why 'trust us' is a necessary but not sufficient credo for public service providers. It is also why external drivers are needed, in the shape of assorted accountability and contestability mechanisms. In a nationalised political culture, these will inevitably come from the centre. Those who pay the money, and who will ultimately be held to political account for what happens with it, will naturally want to exert at least some control over the delivery process. The question is how much, and in what form.

There is a sense in which these mechanisms – of audit, targets, inspection and the like – are surrogates for user power. This does not mean they will be effective mechanisms. The fact that we have the most elaborate system of public service audit, regulation and inspection in the developed world alongside some of the most unsatisfactory public services does not suggest a necessary linkage (except, as some might suggest, in a negative way). We lead the world in public service regulation, but drag behind in the quality of many of our public services. Regulation is indispensable, but it needs to leave enough space for organisations to develop a performance culture of their own, with room to innovate, set priorities and respond to user need.

On target?

As ever, it is a matter of getting the balance right. This is directly relevant to target-setting. All organisations may set targets, but there are key issues about ownership and accountability. An example makes the

The accountability jungle

point. Churches routinely have a board outside with a big thermometer showing their progress towards a fund-raising target. This is a simple target, giving a clear focus for a range of activities. However, not only does the target not define the purpose of the church but it would clearly be absurd if churches in widely different circumstances were set the same target by some higher authority (short of God) or were told how the money raised had to be spent irrespective of particular local needs. Of course there is much more commonality about public services, which is why the 'postcode lottery' charge is always so potent. That is the case for key national entitlements and standards, backed by targets to meet them. However, there is also a case for much more local ownership of many targets (for example, school improvement targets), grounded in particular circumstances and needs, and nourishing a performance culture that involves something more than responding to external demands, with all the gaming, cheating and perverse consequences associated with this.

Yet a shift towards this kind of model would mean taking users seriously, and building them into the process. This has a number of aspects. For example, in current target-setting user involvement is conspicuous by its absence. It should be a requirement for those who set targets for public services to show that users have been fully engaged in the process (which is something more than token consultation). It is likely, for example, that health service users would want ambitious targets for reducing waiting times for treatment; but unlikely that they would want such targets to take precedence over treatment on the basis of clinical priority if there was a conflict. Similarly, it is likely that parents would want schools to have stretching targets for equipping their children with basic literacy and numeracy skills, but unlikely that they would want this to be at the expense of the cultivation of other attributes. It is not just that it is right to involve users, but that it is sensible to do so.

There needs to be effective user involvement in target monitoring too. If public service provider bodies are to have more freedom to set their own targets, then it is essential that they are accountable to someone for both setting and meeting targets that are appropriately stretching, and that user representation should form part of this. There will be no uniform mechanism across the diversity of public services for this purpose, nor should there be. What is appropriate for the NHS may not be appropriate for the school system. What matters is that there should be common principles and objectives.

This raises the whole question of user representation in public services. Thinking in this area remains in a mess, with conflicting approaches in evidence. The 'new localism' seems to promise a reassertion of local democratic governance, but at the same time the creation of a variety of service-specific local boards points in a sharply different direction. New forms of user representation are being introduced in the NHS, but it is difficult to see why new provider organisations (in the shape of foundation trusts) should be thought to require a locally elected element when the key commissioning bodies (the primary care trusts) are thought not to need an elective component. Similarly, although the lack of an elected basis has provided the rationale for user bodies in the NHS, it is not clear why other public services which do have a formal elective basis but in which the user voice is weak (as with local government services) should not also be thought to require forms of direct user representation. We believe that all public services, however provided, should be obliged to have effective mechanisms of user representation.

The prevailing confusions go deeper than this though. A new model of the public service user has begun recently to emerge, as someone armed with information about the performance of different providers as the basis for choice between them. If this really is intended as the direction of advance, especially in the NHS, then it may seem irrelevant to try to build user representation into local health services at all. This model detaches the user from particular local health providers and converts him or her into a consumer of the wider universe of health care. In this model it is necessary only for inspectors and regulators to ensure the basic quality of health provision everywhere and to provide performance data, after which information-rich consumers can exercise their choices. If this really is the direction of travel, then it clearly has radical implications for how we think about local health services (and perhaps other services too).

Confusions and fundamentals

But that is still for the future. For the present it is enough to register the confusions, and explore the implications of different approaches. There are already confusions about the purpose of published performance information about public services, especially when presented in the form of league tables. All organisations need good performance data, and public organisations have an obligation to be transparent about their performance (which will soon be underpinned by the new Freedom of Information Act). But how useful is such information to users? It may be indirectly useful, in so far as it encourages providers to improve their performance, but its direct usefulness is often very limited. It is difficult, if not impossible, for users to move from high-performing to low-performing providers (for example, by deciding to use a different police force), or to convert performance information into effective tools of political accountability. This is emphatically not an argument against such information, but an argument for greater clarity about its purpose. Users also need information that is genuinely useful, which means benchmarking in relation to comparable providers in a form that is easily understood and showing whether an organisation is making progress, going backwards or standing still. For example, schools rightly complain that current league tables do not tell which is a good school and which is a poor one, although this is how the results are often presented.

As well as through direct user representation in particular organisations and services (as with school governing bodies), performance information ought also to serve as part of the armoury of general political accountability. The fact that it does not, except in the crudest way, raises real questions about the present jungle of accountability in Britain. User (or citizen) control can never be effectively exercised unless lines of accountability are clear. It is essential to be able to identify who is responsible for what. Yet this is becoming increasingly difficult, with the result that central government is assumed to be responsible for everything, an assumption that reinforces its desire to control all that it will be held responsible for. This has become the most vicious of vicious circles. Its effect is seen in the daily absurdities of the House of Commons when ministers are asked to account for everything that happens on every Acacia Road in the country.

It is not just that local government has been emasculated over the past twenty years, as the general provider of a range of public services, and turned into a creature of the centre. This process has now reached a point when local government has either to be reinvented or replaced. This takes us beyond our immediate concerns here, but it is nevertheless directly relevant to how users relate to services. Accountability does not work if there is no real responsibility for what is provided, or if responsibility is blurred or disputed (as with the recent argument about responsibility for the shortfall of school funding). It is little wonder that local electoral accountability is in such poor shape, or that most electors have given up on it altogether. This issue is fundamental, and can no longer be dodged. When we reach a point at which most people do not have a clue who is responsible for what, and so settle for making 'the government' responsible for everything, it is time to return to first principles.

It is also more complex than an argument about the general status of local government. Governance arrangements at every level are increasingly variegated and fragmented as the search for more effective delivery models has created a bewildering myriad of organisational forms. This is the world of contractors, partnerships, agencies, quangos and boards, overlaid with all the supporting apparatus of regulation, audit and inspection.[3] Whatever the gains in public management that may flow from this, it opens up real problems about democratic accountability. It is this side of the equation that now cries out for atten-

The accountability jungle

tion. It is scarcely too much to say that most people do not now know who provides the services on which they depend. This makes effective accountability almost impossible, especially when responsibility is anyway divided. It also produces much frustration on the part of users as they struggle to find their way through the accountability jungle.

There is also evidence that this jungle can make delivery more difficult too. In an important recent report on the problem of converting an unprecedented rise in spending on public services into delivering outcomes, the National Audit Office identified the 'complexity of the delivery chain' as one of the key factors:

'These networks often involve complex funding and accountability arrangements, which if not carefully managed, can have an adverse impact on departments' policies to deliver improved services.'

Simplifying lines of organisation and accountability can contribute to better performance. It is worth reminding ourselves that some of the most notable post-war policy successes, such as Harold Macmillan's achievement as housing minister in the 1950s in getting 300,000 houses built in a year, came through straightforward delivery mechanisms and traditional public instructions, and with accountability clearly identified. There is sometimes a danger that the wizardries of the new public management can obscure some very old organisational and political truths.

This is not an argument against new organisational arrangements if these serve the cause of public sector efficiency. But it is an argument in favour of ensuring that clear lines of accountability to users and citizens are not broken beyond repair. If services are disaggregated, then care should be taken to make sure that accountability is firmly re-aggregated. Users need services in which provision is seamless, whatever the internal organisation involved, with unified access points (and advocacy where necessary) and clear accountabilities. This is directly relevant to our argument for Public Service Guarantees too, for in a context where there is a diversity of suppliers it is essential to be clear about who takes responsibility for a service guarantee. Nor should the importance of effective complaint and redress mechanisms be underestimated. It is essential that, however services are organised, users should have access to integrated and straightforward means of having their complaints properly investigated, following a complaint wherever it leads. From an organisation's point of view, user complaints should be seen as a source of continuous quality checking.

This is unfortunately not always the case. Some public services (schools for example, and universities) still do not have proper complaint mechanisms at all. The user of a public service is entitled to have complaints about unsatisfactory service properly investigated. Without the alternative of moving to a different supplier, effective complaint and redress systems for public service users are indispensable. As these are fundamental to how users evaluate public services, they should also be fundamental to how such services are inspected and audited. This is not presently the case. Tracking a 'user's journey' through a public service, or cluster of services, is likely to produce a more genuinely evaluative assessment than merely measuring a number of quantifiable indicators than can easily be measured. This is one aspect of putting user evaluation and satisfaction at the centre of public service assessment (as with the systematic tracking of user satisfaction with the whole range of public services in Canada's Citizens First programme).

Towards a user approach

We now want to take a step back for a moment, as a prelude to proposing a step forward, and offer some observations on the current reform debate about public services, especially in relation to the role of users. We suggested earlier that a number of different directions were in evidence, and that there was a lack of overall coherence of approach. This can be very confusing to all concerned. There does not need to be a uniformity of approach, but there does need to be coherence about the diversity. The Blair Government deserves huge credit for changing the terms of political trade in Britain so that public services are at the top of

The accountability jungle

everyone's agenda. Not only that, along with the extra funding, but the new focus on outcomes – what comes out in terms of achievements as opposed to what merely goes in as resources – represents a major advance on previous positions. Yet there is now a real sense of having arrived at a strategic crossroad. There is no shortage of directions on offer – 'targets', 'choice', 'competition', 'diversity', 'localism', 'autonomy' and many more – but uncertainties about which one(s) to take. What does a user approach suggest?

It suggests, whatever else, that it is necessary to be clear about means and ends, and not to confuse one with the other. What users of public services want are quality services, providing reliable standards when they are needed. In this sense those who argue that quality, not choice, is what matters are right. If that is better secured by collective planning, then it would be a mad perversion of ends and means not to provide it in that way. Alternatively, if mechanisms such as provider diversity, choice and competition can contribute to service quality, then it would be foolish not to employ them. As with so much else, being ideological about ends does not mean being dogmatic about means, or at least should not.

This helps us to think about centralism and localism. The case for centralism is that it reflects the fact that public service users, in a highly uniform political culture, expect the same services everywhere and that it is the job of the central state to ensure this happens. This approach cuts through the usual rhetoric about 'local needs' and 'what communities want' and drives services firmly from the centre. It sets targets, controls funds, appoints and inspects. It solves the problems of accountability by making the centre responsible for everything. This has attractions from the perspective of users, who at least know whom to blame. However, it comes at a cost. Running everything from the centre in practice becomes impossible, so the accountability really becomes a fiction, and the resulting atrophy of local civic life raises issues of democratic ends as well as means.

A New Social Contract

This pitches us right into the present. The Blair Government clearly wants to begin to decentralise, but the language of 'earned autonomy' still defines the conditions of any new localism. From elected mayors to single-service boards, it searches for new governing mechanisms beyond the conventional structures of local authorities. Yet none seem really to bite. Beyond these instruments of collective democracy, the Government is also busily exploring the mechanisms of individual user democracy, of choice and competition. But are these to be seen as alternatives or complements in relation to the collective mechanisms? Will the move to separate services with their own user representation finally break the traditional structure of local government or (as with the Victorians) eventually prompt calls for its (re)integration? Faced with such questions, it is hardly surprising that there is hesitancy at the crossroads.

Against this background, we want briefly to discuss what we see as some of the key issues in current proposals aimed at strengthening the position of public service users, before adding our own proposal. We focus, first, on ideas for strengthening the collective role of users, from greater scrutiny to more democracy. Second, we look at ideas aimed at individual user empowerment, notably through choice and vouchers. Finally, we argue for a new system of guarantees for public service users. We do not suggest that these different approaches are incompatible, or that a mixture of them is either not possible or desirable, but we do believe that it is sensible to try to think coherently about what they involve.

2| Voice and choice

Finding a voice

Building scrutiny into the provision of public services is one way to strengthen the user voice. Local government's internal structure has recently been reorganised to separate out a scrutiny function. New scrutiny bodies, involving users, are being developed in the health service and in other public services user representatives are being included in panels and boards of various kinds.[4] These are important developments, building on earlier experience such as parent representation on school governing bodies, and need to be strengthened and built on. Good scrutiny makes for good services. There is no single model, nor should there be. Users can be represented by a redefinition of existing roles (e.g. non-executive councillors), by user or quasi-user elections (e.g. parent governors), by electoral college procedures (e.g. the former community health councils), or by appointment (e.g. patients' forums). There is plenty of scope for experiment and innovation. In particular we believe there is a strong case for developing the use of random selection, or lot, procedures to find user representatives. This has been tried successfully by some of the lottery boards and is an innovation that should now be extended more widely. It could be used to assemble local user panels from which representatives could be drawn for particular purposes.

A New Social Contract

We should be enthusiasts for good and constructive scrutiny. A scrutiny function, rooted in users, should be integral to all public services, and the assorted army of scrutineers should receive all the support they need to be effective. As civic disengagement seems to accelerate, those who perform scrutiny functions in our public services – often on an entirely voluntary basis – need to be valued and sustained. They help to remedy the general problem of accountability. These are the unsung foot soldiers of our emaciated civic life. If good public services need good scrutiny, from users and citizens, then the scrutiny function needs to be taken very seriously.

We should not be sniffy about appointment as a method of recruiting user representatives, especially if buttressed by experiments with random selection. We badly need to recruit civic participants from new sources, and beyond the narrow confines of the party system. It is the user experience that needs to be tapped (as Aristotle said, it is the wearer who knows where the shoe pinches) and built in to the structure of all public services. This means vigour and imagination in thinking about how the public appointments process works, how a wider range of people can be represented, and how those recruited for public service can be properly supported in the scrutiny roles that they are called upon to perform.

But is better scrutiny enough? Should we not (instead or as well as) be thinking of more directly democratic forms of user control of public services? If accountability is so elusive and fractured, as argued earlier, then perhaps the answer is to make it more directly visible. Instead of public service users having to find an indirect voice through assorted scrutineers who try to speak on their behalf, perhaps it would be better to equip them with a direct voice through democratic elections. This is the case for directly elected health boards or police authorities (just to take the two most frequently cited candidates). This case is certainly worth exploring further. We should not be deterred in making such exploration by a prevailing civic atrophy that seems to make the prospect of extended electoral participation a chimera. The challenge is

Voice and choice

to make a new civic culture, not merely to operate within the confining infirmities of the present one.

Yet any proposals of this kind have to be seriously argued, and the real difficulties confronted. Any moves in this direction would not remove the need for a continuing scrutiny function to be performed. An elective basis does not solve the problem of continuous accountability (indeed, one study of elected and appointed bodies found that elected bodies took this less seriously than appointed bodies).[5] The idea that only appointed services such as the NHS require formal user representation whereas elected services like local government do not may be impeccable democratic logic but it is also wrong.

However the difficulties do not stop there. Many services require more integration, not less (as with local crime reduction partnerships). If locally elected services are to be free to go their own way, the issue of national standards has to be faced. Could unpopular services and users (e.g. speed cameras, the mentally ill) be ditched in favour of popular preferences? If not, what would be the purpose of going down this road? As the area covered by the new elected boards would make it unlikely for candidates to be personally known to electors, the political parties would naturally seek to colonise these elections and run them as normal local elections. It is difficult to see how this would re-energise the local democratic process, which already provides an elective basis for local services but which is itself clearly in trouble.

This last consideration provides the key. Those who advocate an extension of local democracy to specific services have to confront the critical issue of power and resources. People will not participate in a fiction, which is already the fate of local government. Unless the bodies voted for can exercise real control over the money they raise and spend, all that will be created is a cruel illusion. Far from increasing accountability, it will cloud it even further. Somebody else will always be to blame. If a local community wants to employ more police, it should have a way of doing so, and paying for it. That kind of user control is real; other proposed kinds are not. This is why it is not enough to advocate more local democracy, as a way of strengthening user power in public services, without following the argument through to the only conclusions that are capable of giving it substance.

A matter of choice

A different approach to empowering public service users centres on the question of choice, with the idea of some form of voucher as one familiar version of this approach. The Blair Government has declared that choice is one of its key principles of public service reform, and is busily exploring how to give content to this commitment in its particular proposals. In a recent major speech on public service reform, Mr Blair could not have been clearer about the direction of travel: 'It is choice with equity we are advancing. Choice and consumer power as the route to greater social justice not social division'.

What are we to make of this? Is the embrace of choice in the context of public services to be seen as a lamentable capitulation to a neo-liberal agenda, or as a bracing attempt to open up radical political and intellectual territory? The thinking behind the embrace has a number of ingredients. It is argued that people who are used to being treated as consumers in the rest of life, exercising choices about money and services, are no longer content simply to be the passive recipients of whatever kind of services the state provides ('one size fits all' as this has come to be described). A development of this argument is the proposition that if the middle classes are not to detach themselves from the collective provision of health and education then these services have to become much more consumerist, with choice as a key component of this. However, there is a further argument of a rather different kind. This says that choice can be a useful device to drive up the quality of public services, as providers have to strive to meet the needs of consumers (or their purchasers) who can take their business elsewhere. This is choice as means rather than end.

All this suggests that we had better be clear what kind of 'choice' we are talking about, and how it might operate in particular cases. For

Voice and choice

many on the political left choice is a dirty word, the mere mention of which is guaranteed to trigger an instinctive recoil of distaste ('an obsession of the suburban middles classes' Roy Hattersley called it in The *Guardian*). They know it is incompatible with equity, and an alien importation into the state from the unequal world of consumer capitalism. They also know it is usually a fiction in the context of public services anyway (in reality, schools choose children, not parents the schools), and any extension of the concept will merely further advantage the already advantaged at the expense of the disadvantaged. On this view what people really want (and need) are universally good public services, not the chimera of choice. This will be secured by collective political choice and implemented by the traditional machinery of the state.

The danger is that these rival arguments are simply conducted past each other, without really engaging. The critique of choice, as part of the whole neo-liberal box of tricks, is a powerful one. When applied to public services, as with the Conservative Party's recent proposals on health and education, choice can provide a convenient (though extremely expensive) device to move more people from the state to the private sector. It does make sense to emphasise the centrality of collective choice for key aspects of life. These are matters for political decision, through the mechanisms of democracy, and the state is the arena of collective choice. This is why it is important that there is a proper range of choice, through competing political parties offering real alternatives. We rightly value the choices that a market economy gives us, but we also want to exercise choices that a market economy does not give us (which includes the choice about how far market principles should extend). This is why it is right to resist the subversion of citizen by consumer.

When all this is properly said, though, the danger is that it relieves us of the need to think critically about how the state actually works, and whether there are ways in which it might work better. Merely to defend the state against the market, or even to celebrate the wider public domain, is not enough. The real challenge is to combine a defence of the principle of collective provision of key services with a relentless determination to ensure that these services really do meet the needs of those who use them. As we argued earlier, there is nothing in the conception of citizenship that precludes a proper attention to the consumers of services. In the same way, the idea that collective choice makes unnecessary any concern with individual choice is unsatisfactory. It is not enough to say that choice is necessarily incompatible with equity; the real task is to explore whether certain kinds of choice could be used in the service of equity. This is the case made by those who espouse progressive versions of the voucher idea for education, in which poor parents get more valuable vouchers. One such version, in the form of Positive Discriminatory Vouchers (PDVs), was advocated during the dark days of Thatcherism by Julian Le Grand,[6] who is now advising Downing Street on choice. It is far more useful to consider whether such schemes, using choice to advance equity, might actually work than to dismiss all mention of vouchers as irredeemably right-wing. Some are anyway already in use (for example, to buy community care) and give more control to users over the services they receive.

Equity and choice?

The challenge is to develop practical models of public service choice that do pass the test of equity, and which empower people who are currently disempowered. There are some very radical versions of choice available. For example, it is well established that house prices command a substantial premium in the catchment areas of popular schools, areas that are already likely to be relatively advantaged. Instead of simply lamenting the way in which this makes a nonsense of school choice for poorer families, it is more useful to develop a model of school choice that overcomes this problem. Why should geographical proximity (or even an existing child in a school) be thought to trump other claims to a place? When we are developing choice models for public services like health, so that people are not locked into a single local supplier, it seems

Voice and choice

odd not to seek to open up school choice. It would be perfectly possible to have a system in which applications for school places (certainly for secondary schools) were decided upon randomly, so that everyone had an equal chance to get a place in a popular school, with positive effects on other schools too. There would certainly be objections to this, especially from beneficiaries of the present arrangements, but it is an example of a radical choice model.

It is difficult to see why there should be objections to attempts to give more power to the users of public services, both individually and collectively. It is not necessarily a zero sum game, in which you either have individual power or collective power but not both. Enabling patients to choose whether they wish to wait a shorter time for their operations by using different hospitals, or having a choice of where they wish to be treated, strengthens individual choice without undermining collective choice. The Government is right to want to move the NHS in this direction, and to extend the current pilot schemes. The operation of choice also requires the existence of spare capacity, and this is where the collective choice involved in providing extra funding for the NHS enables individual choice to begin to be possible.

This does not mean that all choice is good, or that it may not be deployed to provide exit routes from public services rather than more clout for users of them. In some versions of choice, equity can be a casualty and individual choices can undermine collective choices. However, there is nothing inevitable about this and other versions are available. We should explore these, both because choice can give power and because the exercise of this power can help shape services around the preferences of users, and so improve quality. Those who believe in collective provision of key public services have an obligation to ensure that they understand the vices as well as the virtues of monopoly providers. There is a serious debate to be had about choice and diversity, involving critical exploration of possible models. An engagement in that debate is one choice at least that we should be prepared to make.

A New Social Contract

We want to suggest a rather different approach, but there is no doubt that the voucher model of user empowerment does have a theoretical simplicity. Instead of the state providing services, it provides people with the money to 'buy' services for themselves. At a stroke it transforms the relationship between provider and user. Providers only survive if users want to employ their services, and new providers are encouraged to enter the field. It does not require the state to be good at providing services, only to produce money (which it is good at, from its monopoly position). It recognises the fact that most people are not attached to state services for their publicness and would like to be able to buy a better education for their children or health care when they want it, if public provision is unsatisfactory.

This is a radical model of the state as enabler rather than provider. Unfortunately, its theoretical elegance is not matched by its practical application. Although its appeal to those who wish to roll back the state is obvious, it presents real difficulties for everyone else. Unless the proposition is, say, that the state will fund an expensive private education for every child, with more funding for those with extra needs, then in practice it becomes at best a subsidy to sections of the middle class. Whatever else our education system needs, this is scarcely the priority. Nor is it clear how a universal voucher system would actually work, or how we would get from here to there, not least because schools (and other public services) do not open or close like burger bars. Then there is the individualistic fallacy, the belief that the public interest is merely the summation of individual preferences. A glance at transport policy, in which individual preference to drive cars runs up against the need for a transport system that works, is enough to make the point about the contradictions of individualism. This is not an argument against sensible experiments with voucher systems in certain circumstances, but it does demand that theoretical elegance is matched by serious engagement with the real world.

Voice and choice

Innovation and improvement

Our approach is different. We believe in public services, as services that we have decided by collective democratic choice to organise on non-market principles so that everyone can have access to them and because they are too important to be left to the market. Public services get the task of doing society's tough jobs, which is why simplistic private sector comparisons are frequently so unhelpful. We believe in an ethos of public service, as an approach that incorporates the principles of what a public service is and expresses this in how it operates. We believe that public services require proper funding from collective taxation, with the wealthy paying more into the common pot and the needy taking more out of it. We recite such beliefs because they are fundamental, marking out different approaches to the state and the market. However, the argument should not stop there, although it frequently does.

In particular, for progressives, it is not enough simply to defend the state. The task should always be to improve it. Those who believe in the state, for the kind of reasons given above, have a special obligation to ensure that it works well for those who depend upon it. It is not enough to defend the principle of public service; it is the conversion of that principle into daily practice that really matters. This is why some of the most interesting thinkers on the left in the past have been those (like G.D.H. Cole) who have sought to combine an adherence to public service principles with an aversion to bureaucratic statism. This has involved a search for organisational forms in which users have real control and power, and in which accountability is more than a remote fiction.[7] Our view is that we have to renew that search now.

This means being willing to experiment with forms of direct user control of services, especially at the community level. Schemes such as Sure Start have been innovative in the way they have brought users on to the boards, with real power to shape the services provided, and this creates a quite different relationship between provider and user. Such innovations need to be built on, and carried further. Again, there is no single model, but plenty of scope for trying out different approaches.

A New Social Contract

This is the state as enabler, funder and franchiser rather than direct provider, not because the state needs to be rolled back but because the user needs to be rolled forward. There are real issues about risk, audit and regulation involved in any move in this direction, and new kinds of relationship to be developed between service professionals and users, but these are not insurmountable. Contracting out should come to mean something more than simply hiving off public functions to the private sector.

There are other reasons why moves in this direction need to be explored. All the signs are that the people who pay taxes want to have more connection with what they are spent on. Whatever the general arguments about taxing and spending, it is clear that there is less public willingness to trust the state to deliver service outcomes with the income it receives and greater public inclination to have some linkage between what is paid in and what comes out. This should have been exploited more in the case of health, beyond the linkage between the national insurance increase and the increase in health spending, in the direction of a health insurance tax. More generally, it requires governments to publish an Annual Performance Report, validated by the National Audit Office and Audit Commission, in which levels of taxing and spending are converted into the performance of services provided by the state.

We must not confuse the general arguments about taxation, such as the obvious difficulties of combining a desire for American levels of tax with the demand for European levels of public services, with the particular argument about the need for much more transparency, connection and accountability in the fiscal relationship between the state and its citizens. Indeed, it may well be that the outcome of the general argument about taxation will depend heavily upon the extent to which those who pay taxes come to feel a more direct connection between the paying in and the getting out.

3| Public Service Guarantees

This brings us back to the idea of a contract between the state and its citizens, and the need to make the nature of this contract far more explicit than it has been in the past. This in turn leads to our main proposal, which we believe is the most promising way to think about the next phase of public service development. It builds on existing elements in the Government's public service reform programme, but brings these together in a way that has more direct meaning for the users of public services. What we propose is an explicit system of Public Service Guarantees (PSGs), in which for each service the state spells out what the user is entitled to expect and, by extension, what happens if this entitlement is not met. It is in this sense that we talk of a shift from targets to rights, and about turning public service reform on its head.

Beyond the Citizen's Charter

In some ways we want to carry on where the Major Government's Citizen's Charter programme left off.[8] That was a first attempt to begin to specify what the state was promising to public service users. At the time Labour could not decide whether to dismiss it as a cosmetic irrelevance or to claim authorship of it in local government, so it did both. The programme was certainly full of confusion, on which it eventually floundered, as it struggled to decide whether it was about standards and entitlements or aims and aspirations. It therefore raised expectations without being able to meet them, while its purpose was clouded by its association with a wider political project to diminish the public sphere. Yet for all that it took a Brixton boy to grasp that public service reform involved users knowing what the state promised to deliver, and not just in the generalised way in which this was usually described.

The basic idea behind the Citizen's Charter was, in itself, laudable. In a speech in March 1991, John Major introduced the gist of the concept: 'People who depend on public services – patients, passengers, parents, pupils, benefit claimants – all must know where they stand and what service they have a right to expect.' Individual charters for public services were published setting out commitments on the level and quality of service that users of those public services were entitled to. Some of these charters in effect codified existing rights, such as the tenant's charter which contained recognised rights like the right to security of tenure and the right to repair. Charters for other public services enabled the Government formally to set out commitments on service delivery, including guaranteed waiting times for treatment in the patient's charter or, for parents, rights to information about their children's educational progress and school performance. Service charters were also supposed to explain how users could complain, and what redress they could expect, if service standards fell short. As the Major Government's white paper on the Citizen's Charter explained, the three key elements of the Charter initiative were the provision of standards, information and redress.[9]

The actual implementation of the Citizen's Charter programme, however, failed to realise this vision of responsive public services. The suspicion was that the Citizen's Charter was really more about public relations than public service reform, as little evidence of improved public services could be attributed directly to the Charter initiative despite its high public profile. Charter standards were often too vague to be meaningful, displaying a confusion between enforceable standards and non-enforceable aims or policy objectives. An initial audit in 1994 by the *Financial Times* pointed to this weakness, as well as the limited extent of compensation that had actually been made to

Public Service Guarantees

aggrieved users. More fundamentally, the Institute of Public Policy Research concluded in 1996 that, after five years of operation, the Citizen's Charter had not fulfilled its primary purpose of allowing people to find out about their entitlements and hence to claim them.[10]

When Labour came to office in 1997, it initially adopted a different approach. It was sternly centralist, believing that the task was to use all the governing instruments at its disposal to yank up the performance of public sector institutions, which the Government had identified as its central political purpose. In a key respect this was a major advance on historic Labour approaches to public services, which had been lamentably inattentive to the performance outcomes that spending on these services produced. The whole PSA (Public Service Agreement) system constructed by the Treasury, with its battery of targets and performance monitoring, was designed to link money to performance in a more systematic way. It has real achievements to its credit, but it is irredeemably top-down. It imposes a discipline on public service providers, but its relationship to public service users is necessarily only indirect (through the promise of measurably improved performance).

There is much discussion now about whether the discipline is too tight, and developing attention to some of the costs and limitations of this approach. It seems likely that some rebalancing of the target and regulatory regime will result, with increased ownership of targets by those who have to employ them and a more 'strategic' approach to regulation. Beyond this, though, and more directly relevant to our argument here, there is a developing interest in dealing directly with the service user in terms of expectations and entitlements. It is this approach that we want to see developed further and more coherently. Already in certain parts of the NHS, patients are guaranteed treatment at an alternative hospital if they have waited more than six months for surgery. The cardiac patient choice initiative provides the choice of faster treatment at another hospital to patients who have waited over six months for heart surgery. In London, the option of moving to an alternative provider was initially offered to patients waiting more than

A New Social Contract

six months for cataract surgery, and has since been extended to patients in a variety of other specialities. The guarantee of treatment for those who have waited longer than six months for elective surgery, through offering patients the choice of different hospitals or other providers, is now being implemented throughout the entire NHS. Not only does this approach reconnect with the direction of travel of the Citizen's Charter, but it goes further by more precisely pinning down user entitlements.

This is what our proposal for Public Service Guarantees does in a more systematic way, across the board. It starts with the user, not the provider, and spells out what service entitlement exists in as precise a way as possible. We want to see published PSGs for all services, together forming a citizen's handbook of entitlements. Merely bringing together existing entitlements – for example, to free education until 18, or most health care without payment – would provide a formidable inventory of what the tax-funded state provides for its citizens. However, the challenge now is to go further and, wherever possible, to convert such general guarantees into more specific statements about service availability and quality. Having a guarantee to a poor service is not a guarantee worth having.

PSAs and PSGs: Making the link

What is also crucial, though, is for the system of Public Service Guarantees to be firmly anchored into the Government's overall programme of public service reform. Otherwise, it could drop off the agenda as the Citizen's Charter did once initial enthusiasm for it waned. We suggest giving PSGs equal weight to the Government's existing system of PSAs. Despite the centralist, top-down nature of PSAs and their targets, few would dispute the need to have national targets of some description (complemented by local targets responsive to local conditions and the views of service providers). Overall targets are essential so that the Government can indicate what outcomes and standards of delivery are expected from public services. What we propose is to add in the missing element by introducing Public Service Guarantees

Public Service Guarantees

that indicate to users what standards of service delivery they can expect at an individual level. Public Service Agreements are the logical home for the Public Service Guarantees, given that the original impetus behind the PSAs was to demonstrate to the public what would be delivered in return for their investment in public services.[11]

The particular approach adopted in formulating Public Service Guarantees will clearly differ greatly among services. What is applicable to the NHS will not be applicable to policing, but the obligation will be the same. In many respects the NHS provides the model, as it is possible to specify acceptable treatment times for particular conditions and to convert these into patient entitlements. Existing PSA targets for the NHS already specify service guarantees to patients, such as targets on maximum waiting times for inpatient treatment and guaranteed access to primary care within a certain time period. It would be relatively simple to set out a complementary set of Public Service Guarantees that reflected commitments already made to NHS patients in PSA targets and national service frameworks. Other services will need to adopt their own approaches. In education, for instance, none of the current PSA targets are expressed in terms of service guarantees. Yet some local authorities publish education service charters that spell out what parents are entitled to expect, such as a guaranteed school place for their child or appropriate provision for children with special education needs. The parent's charter that emerged as part of the original Citizen's Charter likewise contained certain rights for parents, including the right to information on their child's progress and to influence how their child's school is run.

Hence, all services should be required to specify the entitlements that they are offering users. If these entitlements are not met, then something should happen. What marks out a guarantee from an aspiration (or a target, or even a standard) is that it is a hard currency as far as users are concerned. Unless this is taken seriously, it would be better not to embark on this path at all. This is why we suggest incorporating Public Service Guarantees in the performance monitoring framework of the

PSAs. PSA targets are serious commitments on public service delivery, for which the Government is held accountable should they fail to be met. An equally serious commitment to upholding user entitlements to service provision would see PSGs form part of PSAs. The form that PSGs would take would be a clear statement of the level or quality of service that users can expect, coupled with a precise account of the redress that users would be entitled to should the guaranteed level of service not be reached.

Embedding Public Service Guarantees in the framework of public service agreements ensures that ministers and departments can be held accountable for failure to meet service guarantees. This explicit link between users' experience of public services and public accountability for them directly addresses one of the major shortcomings of the Citizen's Charter: that it treated users as consumers rather than citizens. (The Citizen's Charter's narrow and individualistic view of citizens as consumers in the public services 'market' was tellingly denoted by the fact that it was a 'Citizen's Charter' rather than a 'Citizens' Charter'.) A more expansive view of public service users as citizens might also encourage user involvement in developing and setting Public Service Guarantees, perhaps by publishing PSGs in draft form and putting them out for public comment and consultation. What is more important, though, is that the Government takes citizens' entitlements to public services seriously by demonstrating that it will be held to account if it does not uphold its end of the social bargain.

Enforcement and redress

As we have seen, it is not enough to specify entitlements unless it is clear what happens if they are not met. In this sense they are triggered by service failure. When a patient cannot be treated within a guaranteed period, then there should be an ability to go elsewhere for treatment and, if necessary, have it paid for. As we have seen, there are already moves in this direction in the NHS. The task is to extend these within the NHS, but also to apply the principle to other services. If the state

Public Service Guarantees

cannot provide a guaranteed service, then it should be expected to provide the money to provide the service. In the case of education, for example, parents and children have a right to expect that the state will provide a satisfactory education for them. In those cases where this does not happen, because a school is consistently failing, then the guarantee is broken and parents should be provided with the means to find schooling elsewhere (for example, in Florida special provision for school choice comes into play if a school is repeatedly judged to be failing. Parents of children at a failing school can either opt to transfer their children to a better-performing public school, or to receive education vouchers enabling them to attend a private school).

This approach differs from universal voucher schemes because it is not aimed at providing subsidised pathways out of public services. It is because we are attached to the principle of public services that we want to strengthen user attachment to them by, as far as possible, explicitly guaranteeing what they provide. Only where there is failure to provide a guaranteed service would the question of redress or alternative provision arise. New providers would have the opportunity to respond to failures, not to undermine success. This approach complements, from the user end, all that the Government is already doing to improve the performance and capacity of public services. The more that the Government's programme is successful, then the more solid will be the service guarantees that it is able to give. Moreover, far from weakening the fiscal role of the state in relation to public services it serves to strengthen it, for the pressure will be on governments to fund services to a level that underpins the service guarantees (or to fund alternatives in cases of failure). In this way, Public Service Guarantees would promote the effective exercise of choice as a means of improving public service delivery. Equally, PSGs would also enhance the ability of those engaged in public scrutiny to assess whether service delivery is meeting commitments made to users. The resulting improvement to the scrutiny function is particularly important given that many public services do

A New Social Contract

not lend themselves to choice-based mechanisms for public service delivery.

There is the issue of the exact status of PSGs and the mechanism by which they are able to be enforced. At all costs, we want to keep the lawyers out of it, so it is not proposed that service guarantees should be legal rights. There are other models available. Here again the example of the Citizen's Charter is instructive. As the charter programme developed, and began to look like a bundle of quasi-rights, the Parliamentary Ombudsman (who investigates complaints about state services) decided that he would regard failures to meet the service standards promised by the Government as 'maladministration', and therefore give rise to a case for redress: 'If [Charter] targets are expressed as mandatory, or a promise has been given that the citizen has an expectation to compensation should they not be met or should they be missed by a specified period, the case for compensatory redress is strong.'[12] This is the right approach, and the appropriate mechanism, as a system of Public Service Guarantees is developed. Independence of investigation and judgement is secured, while the legal bog is avoided.

Redress for failure to meet Public Service Guarantees would be based on the broad principle already adopted by the Ombudsman: that a person who has suffered injustice as a result of maladministration should be back in the same position as he or she would have been had things gone right in the first place. In relation to PSGs, as we have seen from earlier examples, this may mandate the involvement of an alternative service provider or financial compensation for the inability to provide an appropriate level of service. Public Service Guarantees will need to stipulate the nature of the redress that users are entitled to should the guaranteed service level not be reached, so that the Ombudsman is able to recommend appropriate remedies for instances of service failure. In this way, the enforcement of PSGs would be a natural extension of the Ombudsman's role in rectifying maladministration and poor practice in public service delivery. The Ombudsman's existing powers may need to be expanded, however, in order to deal with collective complaints. This would prevent the Ombudsman's office from being overwhelmed by a deluge of similar individual complaints in those situations where many would be affected by the failure to meet guaranteed levels of service provision. It would also enable the Ombudsman more latitude to investigate repeated failure to meet Public Service Guarantees without being limited to the particular circumstances of an individual case.

Where next?

The guarantees can be developed progressively for each service, reflecting their distinctive characteristics. They also offer an opportunity to link obligations to rights (for example, to send children to school, to keep NHS appointments), for a contract is an exercise in reciprocity. The key feature is the clarity of commitment that is involved on both sides. Citizens and state should know what is expected of them. In particular, the state will be required to stipulate what are universal commitments, to standards guaranteed everywhere, and what are not; and also what services, or parts of services, are not provided, so that citizens know that they may have to make their own arrangements. This also provides the basis for co-payment systems, in which the respective responsibilities of state and citizen are clearly identified.

We do not claim this is the last word on a scheme of Public Service Guarantees. It is much more of a first word, the beginning of what needs to be a process of refinement and fleshing out. There are key issues and questions still to be tackled. How are service guarantees, across very different services, to be defined? How is the level at which they are set to be determined? What is the process for reviewing the guarantees? When there are several providers who will be responsible for the guarantee? What are the costs likely to be? All such questions require further work. Nor is it being claimed that this scheme somehow dispenses with other approaches to public services that are being developed, which it clearly does not. What it does do, though, is provide a way to bring these approaches together in a coherent focus on the entitlements of those for whom public services are provided.

The proposal for service guarantees sketched out here will not commend itself to two groups of people. It will be disliked by those on the right for whom the ideological task is to roll back public provision of key services. They will not be attracted to an approach that has the potential to strengthen attachment to public services through a more explicit kind of contract. Equally, the proposal will not appeal to those on the left who are content simply to defend the state against the market, or to argue for more taxes and higher spending, but who dislike attempts to insist that the services provided by the state should be assessed in terms of their performance for users. However, it should appeal to all those who believe in the principle of public provision, as an arena of non-market equity, but who also want to know what they can actually expect for their money.

4| Conclusion

It is time to bring the arguments in this pamphlet together. This is best done by thinking of the 3 Rs of public services from the perspective of users: representation, rights and redress. All three are important, and connect together. They provide the key principles against which proposals for strengthening the position of users in relation to particular services can be assessed. We have emphasised the need for development of a rights-based approach, but this sits alongside representation and redress within a wider framework that takes users seriously. Nor should these principles be seen as an alternative to a more straightforward emphasis on the need for quality of service. In our view user representation, rights and redress are essential constituents of quality, as well as routes to its achievement. We offer a concluding word about each.

Representation enshrines the principle that service users should have an effective voice in how a service is provided, including a means by which service providers can be held to account. There is no single model for how this can be secured, and several can be combined. It is not enough for a service to have an elective basis for effective representation to be secured (nor is the absence of an elective basis evidence that user representation is ineffective). There is considerable scope for trying out different mechanisms appropriate to particular services, and at different levels of a service. The only requirement is that channels for user representation should be authentic, not cosmetic, with some real opportunity for influencing service delivery. The reason why 'consultation' so often fell into disrepute was that it failed this test. If users, or their representatives, are to devote time and effort to public services, it will only be because there is some real chance for them to make a difference.

Rights provide the means by which service users can own public services in direct and concrete terms. They convert general claims into specific entitlements, at least in those circumstances where this is possible (and clarify where it is not). It is not necessary or desirable that these should be legal rights, except where (as in some areas already) this is deliberately intended, but it is nevertheless necessary that they should be capable of being enforced. Rights make explicit the contract between the state and its citizens with respect to the provision of public services. The content of such rights will reflect the nature of different public services, and will develop over time, but cumulatively they provide the basis for a new citizen's charter that captures the intention of the original version while overcoming its limitations.

Redress is the cost of poor service. It should be integral to the relation of the state to the users of its services. If a promised service is not delivered, or delivered badly, then an effective mechanism of complaint and investigation should kick in, with the prospect of redress waiting in the wings. This should not be optional, discretionary or arbitrary, but part of a coherent approach to redress across government that acknowledges the costs involved in service failure. In particular, when the rights promised to citizens in particular public services are not met, then it should be clear what the costs to the state are in terms of the nature of the redress that is then provided. Redress ceases to be, at best, an add-on extra to public service provision and becomes integral to the contract between the state and its citizens.

So this is our prospectus for the next stage of public service reform. It switches the emphasis from provider to user, within a framework of representation, rights and redress. In particular it makes the case for the progressive development of a system of Public Service Guarantees, making explicit the entitlements that service users have and what

Conclusion

happens when these are not met. In this sense we make service failure the trigger for more choice and diversity. We reject the arguments of those, on one side, who really want to dismantle public provision and of those, on the other side, who simply want to defend it. The aim should be to improve it. In fact we prefer to think of the continuous development of a performance culture in public services rather than endless talk of 'reform'. We believe that our proposal contributes to this, and builds on what has already been achieved. Making users central merely recognises what public services are for.

In his speech to the *Guardian* public services summit in January 2004, Tony Blair declared that 'the priority for reform – the principle tying together the different elements of change – is to put the public at the heart of public services, making "power to the people" the guiding principle of public sector improvement and reform.' There could scarcely be a better way of putting this principle into practice than by guaranteeing what people are entitled to. This really could provide the basis for a new social contract between the state and citizens.

A New Social Contract

References

1. *On Target? Government By Measurement*, Public Administration Select Committee, Fifth Report of Session 2002-03 (HC 62), 2003; *Targets in the Public Sector*, Audit Commission, 2003; *Strategic Plan 2004-07 Consultation*, Audit Commission, 2003
2. 'A passport to costly healthcare', *Financial Times*, 10 June 2003
3. 'Local Democracy Renewed?' by N Bonney in *Political Quarterly*, Vol 75, No 1, January-March 2004
4. *The Scrutiny Map*, Centre for Public Scrutiny, 2003
5. *Accountabilities: Five Public Services*, P Day and R Klein, Tavistock, 1987
6. 'Rethinking Welfare: A Case for Quasi-Markets?' by J Le Grand in *The Alternative: Politics for a Change*, B Pimlott, A Wright and T Flower (eds), W H Allen, 1990
7. For example, *Consuming Public Services*, N Deakin and A Wright (eds), Routledge, 1990
8. The idea of rights as entitlements to public services was also expressed by G Mather in *Rights and the Free Market: Costed Enforceable Rights for Citizens*, European Policy Forum, 1999
9. *The Citizen's Charter*, Cm 1599, July 1991
10. *Beyond the Citizen's Charter: New Directions for Social Rights*, I Bynoe, IPPR, 1996
11. *Public Services for the Future: Modernisation, Reform, Accountability. Comprehensive Spending Review: Public Service Agreements 1999-2002*, Cm 4181, December 1998
12. *Parliamentary Commissioner for Administration Annual Report for 1993*, Third Report of Session 1993-94 (HC 290), 1994, paragraph 6

Recent Fabian Publications

The Making of Europe's Constitution by Gisela Stuart
Gisela Stuart MP's candid insider's guide to how Europe's draft constitution was written offers a series of radical proposals for engaging the public in EU affairs. Stuart argues we must change the way Britain deals with Europe if we are to contribute fully to the reshaping of European politics.

'Mr Blair should take the advice of Gisela Stuart to reform the way Parliament scrutinises EU decision-making.' *The Independent*

'A fascinating - and courageous - account of the way the constitution was painfully, sometimes secretively, argued, wangled and bullied into its draft form.' *Guardian*

'This pamphlet takes us inside the EU constitution-making process and asks some fundamental questions about it. These have to be faced by all of us, whatever view we take of what is being proposed.' Tony Wright MP, member of the Fabian Executive

December 2003   ISBN 0 7163 0609 3   £6.95

Exploding the Migration Myths by Russell King, Nicola Mai and Mirela Dalipaj (Published with Oxfam GB)
By speaking to migrants themselves, this report identifies the real reasons behind economic migration and what drives those who undertake it. It explores an approach that can maximise its benefits for migrants, their country of origin and their host country.
November 2003   ISBN 0 7163 3059 8   £12.95

Progressive Globalisation: Towards an international social democracy by Michael Jacobs, Adam Lent and Kevin Watkins
This pamphlet argues for the management of global capitalism under social democratic principles. Calling for a new coalition to work for progressive globalisation, it sets out the 'four pillars' of a new global system.
September 2003   ISBN 0 7163 0608 5   £6.95

A Better Choice of Choice: Quality of life, consumption, and economic growth by Roger Levett et al
Four of the country's leading sustainable development thinkers and practitioners argue that consumption must be addressed head on as resource productivity is not keeping up with economic growth and challenge all those interested in how public policy contributes to sustainable development and individual and social well-being.
August 2003   ISBN 0 7163 3058 X   £9.95

The Future of the Monarchy: The report of the Fabian Commission on the Future of the Monarchy
The first comprehensive blueprint for Royal reform for over 300 years, this report examines the key roles and functions of the British sovereign and the Royal Family including constitutional powers, the monarch's relationship with the law, the Church of England and the Commonwealth, and how it is organised and financed.
July 2003   ISBN 0 7163 6004 7   £11.95

Communities in Control: Public services and local socialism by Hazel Blears
Transcending consultation and participation, the author looks at how local communities can own, manage, plan, and benefit from public services. Blears calls for new forms of community interest companies and a Citizen Participation Agency to create a new generation of community activists and leaders.
June 2003   ISBN 0 7163 0607 7 £6.95

Wealth's Fair Measure: The reform of inheritance tax by Ruth Patrick and Michael Jacobs
Inheritance tax avoidance has become too easy, making the tax unfair and virtually voluntary. This publication explores how best it could be reformed, and the problems with the current system.
April 2003   ISBN 0 7163 3057 1 £9.95

Commercialisation or Citizenship: Education policy and the future of public services by Colin Crouch
An analysis of private sector involvement in public service, showing how this threatens the citizenship basis of education. Crouch offers a number of proposals for a strategy of modernising public services in a manner which is compatible with the concept of the welfare state as a fundamental component of social citizenship.
March 2003   ISBN 0 7163 0606 9 £6.95

All's well that starts well: Strategy for children's health by Howard Stoate and Bryan Jones
Britain is becoming a chronically unfit society with one in five adults dangerously overweight and the life expectancy of children being less than our own. Stoate offers a range of possible strategies from guidelines on meal planning to tax incentives to fresh produce suppliers.
December 2002   ISBN 0 7163 0604 2 £6.95

Completing the Course: Health to 2010 by Ray Robinson and Anna Dixon
During the Second Term the Fabian Society has held a series of seminars as part of its Health Policy Forum to provide members of the policy community, politicians and opinion formers with the opportunity to debate the key issues in the long term development of health politics and policy in the UK. This pamphlet provides a comprehensive guide to the current reforms and argues that a period of stability is needed to bring about sustainable service improvements, with greater continuity than has been evident over the last decade.
December 2002   ISBN 0 7163 0605 0   £6.95

The Courage of Our Convictions: Why reform of the public services is the route to social justice by Tony Blair
Acknowledging that tension exists between national audits and inspections and local autonomy, Blair argues that this can be overcome and sets out his four principles of reform: national standards, devolved power, professionalism and choice.
September 2002, ISBN 0 7163 0603 4, £6.95

Paying for Progress: A new politics of tax for public spending
The highly influential report of the Fabian Taxation Commission which argues for a new approach to taxation and the public spending it pays for, arguing that the public must be 'reconnected' to taxes and the public services which these finance. Providing key information on the UK tax system, this text examines a series of reforms possible to meet the goals of social inclusion and environmental protection.
November 2000   ISBN 0 7163 6003 9   £9.95

To order any of the above titles please email bookshop@fabian-society.org.uk or ring 020 7227 4900